Praise for Sticks!

"What a relief to discover *Sticks*! This easy to implement system will literally change your life, and more importantly, your child's life for the better. No matter how old your child is, this is a must-read parenting book. *Sticks* packs a punch - prioritizing the big picture while providing practical tools for day-to-day. A golden gem in a sea of parenting books!"

Catherine P.
Philadelphia, PA

"*Sticks* is a great tool for creating order and margin in our family! I love how I can adapt it to fit our specific needs in different seasons of parenting. I'm thrilled to find a teaching tool that can replace the yelling and the crazy… with much greater results."

Deb K.
Tinley Park, IL

"This book met me right where I am, as a momma of kids ages 8, 6, and 2. It brought me to tears at some points as the history of *Sticks* began at a stage in the author's life that I can truly relate to in my own. We have been yearning for a system like this in our home without even realizing it. I love how *Sticks* encourages a sense of independence and autonomy in my children. I see the structure and game plan becoming part of our family life and can imagine how it will continue to grow with my kids. What a timely blessing! I am eager to start this soon!"

Hayley J.
Phoenix, AZ

"Like many families where both parents work outside the home, our mornings and evenings are typically focused on what needs to be done before heading out the door or before our heads hit the pillow. We have little time to actually enjoy watching our children grow into adulthood. *Sticks* has provided an ingenious way to, not only free-up our time previously spent worrying about the minutia around daily routines, but more importantly providing our children the tools to organize, prioritize and simplify their lives in ways that are meaningful to them. This allows us as parents to provide direction, all the while having the time to enjoy parenthood as it was meant to be. "

Larry K.
Oxford, MS

Sticks!

A Practical Way to Reduce Stress, Improve Discipline,

and

Create the Family You Want

Nadia Swearingen-Friesen

Four Hope
Publishing

Four Hope Publishing
Chicago

Molly, Stick to it! You can do this. Nadia Swearinger Friesen

3

© 2015 by
Nadia Swearingen-Friesen

Editor: Sarah Zylstra
Cover design: Gabe Taviano
Interior Design: Mark Rueben

Swearingen-Friesen, Nadia, 1967-
Sticks! A Practical Way to Reduce Stress, Improve Discipline, and Create the Family You Want/Nadia Swearingen-Friesen
ISBN 978-0-9963538-0-9

All websites and contact information listed herein are accurate at the time of publication, but may change in the future or cease to exist. The listing of website references are for informational purposes and listing does not imply endorsement of their activities.

We hope that you enjoy this book from Four Hope Publishers. Our goal is to provide thought-provoking and encouraging books and products that will empower parents to approach the raising of their children in an intentional and nurturing manner.

Four Hope
Publishing

Chicago, IL

Printed in the United States of America

Without them, I have nothing to say.
Without them, my days may be quiet and neat,
but
fully without purpose.

For this season, they motivate me and fill my
thoughts.
They color the way I see the world and reveal
to me the wonder that I might otherwise miss.

It is the call of my heart to do right by them.

This book is dedicated to my four babies:
Noah, Benjamin, Josiah and Elizabeth
and
to my husband, Mark, who shares my passion,
not only for family,
but for the ones who fill our days.

Contents

Introduction: A Needed Word of Hope

*"I give grace because
I so desperately need it."*
-Lysa Terkeurst

Maybe you picked up this book because you are curious. You may be in a good place yet also find yourself open to new ideas, new motivational methods, new parenting techniques. If so, this book is for you. Sticks can help focus your efforts. But if you've read this far, you may also be weary. If so, this book is *sincerely* for you. I know what it is like to wake up each morning still worn out from the day before. I know what it is like to look into the faces of my sweet children and wonder how we got to this place. I know what it is like to fall into bed, bone-tired, and know that we are just barely getting by. It is overwhelming. But you are not alone.

As I speak to groups around the country, I find myself face-to-face with people just like you, just like me. I can see the fatigue in their eyes. I hear their frustration as they fight through this season of parenting, feeling like they are not giving to their children what they hoped they would. I watch tears well and listen to words spill and I learn, again and again, that this is what parenting can look like if we do not know to choose another way.

There is another way.

So, here you sit with this book before you -- an intentional quick read with lots of details to help you get started. And maybe you feel overwhelmed. Maybe you think this strategy won't work. The truth is that it will not work unless you do it. Nothing changes if we get up each morning and do the same thing we did the day before.

But, our children are growing up. Imagine a poster somewhere that has all the days you will spend raising your children listed on a giant chart. Can you see it? Each day, one number is crossed off in red. Picture, just for a minute, how many days are marked off already! Whether you are reading this with an infant in your arms or living with a teen, you have spent some of your days already. But the flip side is – there are also lots of days remaining. And no matter how it feels, no matter how dark a day becomes, there is hope when we picture the days that remain because it gives us time to change things. Time to embrace and enfold our children, time to teach them and raise them well. But this time is not something to waste. It is a *finite* thing that will run out. So, we cannot ignore their need. We cannot forget our dreams. We cannot go to bed and get back up and do the same thing we have always done that has never worked well.

No, we must try something new.

As you ponder where to begin, I want you to hear this truth. If you never follow this book's advice, if you never create a system, if you set this all down and do nothing more than remember what you wanted to offer your children before they were ever born, you are light-years ahead of the curve. Because the reality is that we get so busy with the day-to-day living of our day-to-day lives that we honestly forget that we once dreamed of *a life* for our family. We get so tired, so worn down, that we begin to believe that what life really looks like is just getting by. So please, take a few minutes to remember. Before you had children, before all of this, what did you hope you would give? Who did you hope you would be? What type of parent did you want to become before a baby was in your arms? What did you admire about parents you knew and what did you want to avoid?

Take a minute.

Remember.

Let those memories settle in deep because there was something good in all that -- idealistic perhaps, but good. Grab a pencil and write down some thoughts. Because remembering is good, and just thinking it through can help you to come to a place where you feel a new urgency to change. And hopefully, you will also see that some of what you wanted you are actually doing!

Here's the thing. You seriously care about this job. I know you do because there are a lot of books to read in this world and you looked right past great novels and amazing biographies and tantalizing cookbooks to spend time reading this one. You did this because you care deeply about those who have been entrusted to you. You want to do right by them. You want to meet goals. You want to raise them to be amazing adults and loving people and you are willing to evaluate your place in their lives to see if there is more you can do.

That alone is pretty amazing.

So, the path you are on is heading toward hope. You are willing to learn, willing to fight, and willing to move toward what you want.

For them.

For you.

For your family.

Now is the time to begin.

Chapter One: Falling Asleep at the Wheel

"If you want to make your dreams come true,
the first thing to do is wake up."
-JM Power

The problem with falling asleep at the wheel is that you slide quietly into it, only catching yourself after your eyes glaze over and you start to drift a little. It happens when the car is warm and the speed is steady, when your body is comfortable and relaxed. It's a sign that you need to pull over for a cup of coffee or start a lively discussion with your passenger. It's a warning that unless you tweak your behavior, worse things are ahead.

It's the same thing with parenting. You can hit a comfortable speed and drive along for a while on autopilot, until something jerks you awake and you realize your parenting has drifted off-center, has lost its focus.

I jerked awake on an ordinary Wednesday morning. My snuggly two-year-old, who joined me each day long before the sun, greeted me with a pile of books and a sweet, small smile. He climbed into bed with me every morning and whispered, "Read, momma, read," before my eyes were open or I could focus on the storybook words.

When the clock said 7:00 a.m., I settled Josiah with books and blankets and headed down the hall to wake my older boys for school. As I walked past the nursery, I could see that Elizabeth, the youngest of my four, was awake and eager to be freed from her crib. I told her I would be back and focused on the task at hand.

The older boys, Noah and Benjamin, needed to get up for school.

We had not been parents of four for long. The hustle and bustle of our big family was still new to Mark and me, and we were trying to learn the logistics of managing so many. Benjamin and Noah were six and seven, in kindergarten and second grade.

Josiah, my early riser, was two, and Elizabeth had just turned one. Adopted in China, she had been home only a short time.

Caring for all of them was a dream come true for me, even in my fatigue, but the organization it required was not my strongest suit. I had to work at the structure of it, always trying to stay a step ahead of what would be needed next. Even in the struggle of it all, I loved the work before me. Every day had moments of laughter, and I loved being mom to my four.

As I headed down the hall that fateful Wednesday, I remember wondering how it came to be that I had children old enough to go to school, *but not old enough to wake themselves up.* Please, don't misunderstand. I love this work and so want to be a mom who wakes my babies up with a happy little ditty each day. I want to rub their little boy backs and tousle their white-blonde hair and start their day off well. The issue was that they just would not get up.

I didn't know it yet, but the problem was all mine. Because I had taken the responsibility of waking them each day, the job did not belong to them. They played no part in getting up because getting up was something momma did *for* them. Not something *they* did for *themselves.*

And so it began. With my tired voice, I sang a little song. I told them it was time. I explained that the bus would come whether they got up or not. And little by little, my patience was used up. I resorted at last to pulling their feet to the edge of the bunk bed and placing them onto the floor.

In the hallway were piles of clothes chosen for this day. As the boys walked sleepily out of their room, I handed each of them a bundle of clothes and reminded them again about the bus. Whether they were ready or not, it would come. I sent them downstairs to get dressed and returned to the little ones waiting for me.

Picking Elizabeth up, I laid her on the floor, and Josiah came in, too. I changed their diapers, got them dressed, and gave them a book to share. Quickly, I went through my room gathering the books I had read with Josiah earlier and pulling on a t-shirt and yoga pants. Back in the nursery, I loaded a baby onto each hip. It was time to rejoin Noah and Benjamin and get them off to school.

Imagine my surprise when I found my two boys seated comfortably on the living room couch, *undressed.* The clothes they had brought down sat in piles on the floor; our sheltie now using one small pile as a pillow for her head. The television was not on, and they were not speaking to one another at all. They just sat there, two lumps on our sofa, knowing that the bus would be here soon.

In complete shock, I looked at my boys and said, "What are you *doing*?!"

In absolute slow-motion, they turned and looked at me, expressionless. Benjamin spoke first.

"What?" he wondered aloud. "What's the matter?"

I couldn't even pretend to be calm and loving. "What are you *doing*?" I yelled. "Why aren't you getting dressed? The bus will be here shortly and you are going to miss it! You have not yet started breakfast! *Why* aren't you getting dressed?"

And then came the words I know I will always remember. Benjamin, in a momentary lapse of reason, calmly spoke the words that would forever change his life.

"Because," he said, *"you didn't tell us to."*

Even in that moment, I have to tell you, those words repeated themselves in my head. *Because you didn't tell us to....* My smart, loving, eager, curious, compassionate, active, and athletic boys did not get dressed because I didn't tell them *specifically* to do so. They must have known it was necessary to take off their pajamas in order to get ready for school, but we were raising them in such a way that even though they knew it, they would not act until I told them to act. It was in this moment, on an ordinary Wednesday morning, that I knew I had fallen asleep at the wheel. I had lost sight of my parenting goals entirely.

When my husband, Mark, and I got married, we sat and dreamed of the day when we would have a family of our own. We dreamed about having children, both biological and adopted. We talked about what we wanted for them and what we thought our parenting style would look like. We talked about how we would like to raise children in a loving environment built on a solid belief system. We talked about the vital role our faith would play in our daily lives. We talked about how important it would be to raise children knowing that they would *become adults*. Our time with our children would be short, but we wanted to be sure that we were intentional about what we would give to them during that time.

And yet, somehow, over the years, much of that had fallen away. The day-to-day tasks that filled our waking hours had come to *run us*, and all that we had hoped for seemed a distant thought in the midst of so much busyness. School, preschool, and playdate schedules came together daily with our own work, church, and volunteer schedules in a way that left little time for the very things we knew we valued most. In the end, it seemed, we spent less time working on all that we had hoped to give to our children, and more time just working. We had lost our way and landed in a place where we were just getting by. Get up. Get by. Get to bed. Repeat.

And so it came to be that my children had no alarm clock and no reason to think about what should happen on a Wednesday morning, no sense about what it means for the bus to have to wait for them. And so it came to be that all their responsibility had become my own, added to all the details and tasks that already fell to me. And so it came to be that I did not wake my children with a smile or with a happy little ditty, but with a voice of exhaustion and frustration at 7:00 a.m.

Benjamin had shown me all of this by speaking one short, telling sentence. Little did he know that his simple words on an ordinary

Wednesday morning would change not only his world, but our family life, as well.

On that Wednesday morning, "Sticks" was born.

Parenting Pause:

1. What areas of your family life are causing stress?

2. If you could change something about your home life, what would that be?

3. In what areas do your children need additional teaching in order to accomplish tasks independently?

Chapter Two: Thinking it Through

"And what might seem to be
a series of unfortunate events,
may, in fact, be the first steps
in a journey."
-Lemony Snicket

After that worrisome Wednesday, I became much more aware of the things we were missing, of the goals we had lost. But where do you go from there? Once you see and understand a problem, the solution is not always easily found.

For weeks, I thought through methods that could help us find our way. Having worked in many fields, I hoped some bit of my own life experience might offer a solution. I started with my college years, when I worked at a Christian camp. While thinking through those experiences, I recalled a lot about grace, a lot about love, a lot about being present with kids … but that wasn't the answer I was seeking. Was it?

Moving past my life at camp, I rifled through teaching materials from a season long gone-by. As a primary teacher in an elementary school, I remembered the wonder of structure, the security in predictability, the importance of teaching well enough that students would internalize the lessons and store them up to be built upon later. All of this was good … but it wasn't the answer I was seeking. Was it?

After my years as a teacher, Mark and I felt called back to the college campus. This time we were not students, but found ourselves living there as I worked as a residence director. The job was living and working with college students while teaching them the life lessons they needed to become successful adults. As I processed this experience, I recalled the value we placed upon relationships and goal-setting and community. I remembered how important it was to respect the students right where they were and yet have an eye on where they needed to go. We had to hold that vision for them when they were unable to see it themselves. All of it important … but it wasn't the answer I was seeking. Was it?

Each of these experiences held a lesson for me, a lesson for my children, which helped me to remember what they needed from us. My children needed the love and grace I had showered on my campers. They needed the structure, predictability, and teaching I had created for my first grade classroom. My children needed the focus on goals, the comfort of community, and the lessons on relationship-building that we had offered our college students. They needed someone to hold the vision, not only of who they were, but of who they might become. But how did we give them what they needed in a practical, daily way?

Mark and I replayed Benjamin's words in our heads as we sought to get back on track. We wanted to make a list of goals that were tied to those things we had once wanted-- those things I had learned in camp cabins, in classrooms, in college residence halls. We wanted to choose a direction for our family that would correct our path and bring us closer to the dreams we had for our children.

The first thing that became clear to us was that our children relied too heavily on us to know just what to do. Even tasks repeated daily would be left undone without a verbal reminder. We knew it increased the frustration in our home and did not prepare our children for responsible living in the future. Neither Mark nor I were told each day what we had to do. Instead, we had an internalized list of daily activities that we did because they needed to be done. Even very young children can keep track of simple jobs, like putting on clothes, finding socks, and cleaning up toys. Yet our school-aged children would not get dressed without being expressly told to do so. We needed to help them learn to internalize their tasks and take responsibility for age-appropriate activities.

The next thing that we wanted to tackle was the exasperation we felt on a daily basis. We knew we were not alone but could not accept that being frustrated is a normal part of parenting. We allowed ourselves to dream a bit. What would life look like if we didn't yell? What would it feel like if we never nagged? Nagging feels awful for parents, feels awful for kids, and almost never works. It is the most pointless attempt at discipline I have ever used, yet we were doing it every day. Mark and I wanted to be parents who didn't yell and nag. Living in frustration had brought us to this place. We needed to let ourselves out.

A lot of the angst we acted upon was created by the way we were micromanaging each of our young kids. It felt like we were a part of everything they did and that none of it would happen apart from our help. Because we were totally intertwined with their minutiae, we were often locked in a power-struggle over some less-important point.

"Eat your vegetables."

"Pick up your toys."

"Apologize to your sister."

We were engaging in these battles instead of teaching the importance of what we requested, and because of this, found ourselves in frequent stand-offs when our children would dig in their toes and refuse. We wanted them to have healthy lives, good relationships, musical experiences, a desire to read—and yet, we were coming close to losing these things because we insisted that it happen *our way.* Was there any way to encourage our kids to take charge of these helpful and enriching aspects of life? Micromanaging was getting us nowhere. There had to be another approach.

As we became increasingly aware of areas where our children needed guidance, we also began to notice that they were not as close to one another as we hoped they would be. Our older two boys played beautifully together, growing up more like twins than boys who are a year and a half apart. Our younger two children also got along well, contentedly sharing toys and games. Though all of this led to a peaceful house, we were missing something important. The older boys and the younger kids really didn't play together. Ever. Our children only played with the sibling with whom they were close in age. But we wanted more. We wanted *all* our children to share a deep bond that would far outlast either Mark or me. We wanted them to build solid relationships with each other so that when they were older and times were hard, they would always have family to fall back on for support. We wanted *all* of them to connect, to communicate, to understand one another, and to grow closer as they grew older.

As Mark and I studied our family, we knew that life could be better than it was. We loved remembering what we wanted, and we were comforted by the picture of what we could become. And yet, knowing what we wanted would not bring us to that place. We needed a plan.

Knowing this was half the battle.

Parenting Pause:

1. What life experiences might help you address frustrating areas in your family life?

2. Make a list of the family characteristics or goals you felt were important before you had children. Do you still feel these things are important? Are you tending to them today?

3. What do you wish you were able to do with and for your family today?

Sticks Resources:

Mark and I took a lot of time to remember the goals we had for our family. We were missing the mark on many of these. When we evaluated our family life to prepare for needed change, we realized that these were the goals we were not meeting:

- Take responsibility: We wanted kids who were responsible and took care of their own daily tasks.

- Make healthy choices: We wanted our kids to learn to live healthy lives, which we defined as being active each day (playing outside, participating in sports) and choosing healthy food.

- Be well-rounded: We wanted our children to be involved in music and reading each day.

- Delay gratification: We wanted our kids to know what they value and then to work toward it. We did not want to buy them the desires of their hearts for no reason. Birthday and Christmas gifts are great, but throughout the rest of the year, we wanted our kids to earn their toys.

- Play together: We wanted our kids to build good relationships with one another but realized that this is rarely taught. Since they will likely have each other longer than they will have us, we made this a priority

- No shouting required: We did not want to be parents who yelled to communicate. But the stress in our home had led us to that place.

- No nagging required: Nagging feels bad to the nagger, feels bad to the nag-ee, and does not work. Why do we do it?

- A daily standard: Whether we were distracted or not, we wanted certain things (teeth brushing, pet feeding, homework finishing) to happen daily.

These were our goals. What are yours?

Chapter Three: Sticks!

"The secret of change is to
focus all of your energy
not on fighting the old,
but on building the new."
-Socrates

Having spent years as a first grade teacher, I know I am supposed to say that sticker charts are the most amazing teaching tools. And the truth is, I did use them in the classroom, and they worked well. But at home, it began to feel like we had a sticker chart for everything. They were in the kitchen for putting away silverware, in the bathroom for going potty, and in the bedroom for straightening up. And honestly, none of it was working!

There were many problems with this method, not the least of which was that the responsibility for the system sat with me. I had to remind them to do their chore, stick around while they did it, and then peel off a sticker and guide them while they put it on the right square. All of this took a lot of time, and a lot of patience. And while it isn't hard for me to be patient with my children when I am teaching them something new, it's much more difficult to be patient when the lesson never seems to be learned, the responsibility never passed over to them. The monotony and inefficiency were wearing me out. If I was going to teach my children to be more responsible in age-appropriate ways, clinging to the path that led us here was not the way to do it.

One morning after the older boys left for school, I found myself sitting at the kitchen table thinking about the problem at hand. On the table sat Noah's nearly completed school project, a building made of Popsicle sticks. We had purchased hundreds of these inexpensive craft sticks to ensure that we would have enough to complete his work. I was absent-mindedly running my hand through the box of sticks when suddenly, it all became abundantly clear. I could use these sticks!

I wanted to build a system that would be inexpensive, accessible, child-friendly, and adaptable. Using Popsicle sticks met all of these criteria!

Looking around the kitchen for other helpful supplies, I happened upon a stack of plastic cups from restaurant kids' meals. We have so many of these cups from years of parenting that my husband literally begs me to leave them on the table after we eat out. I have to take them with me, though, because they're so handy for outside play, crafts, or even to splash in the tub. Now, with sticks in one hand and cups in the other, I was about to find a new purpose for both.

My mind was reeling now, and I was excited as I grabbed a piece of paper and folded it into fourths. I started by labeling each section with a name. Noah, Benjamin, Josiah, Elizabeth -- each had daily tasks. I brainstormed these onto the sheet and made sure the list was not limited to chores alone. Instead, it included everything I could think of, each activity that they did every day. As parents, there are many things we tell our kids to do daily that they already know must be done. What if we *never* had to say it again? What if they knew to brush their teeth, make their bed, get dressed, put on shoes, eat breakfast, read a book, play outside, play with a sibling--and we never had to say a word? What if they actually did all these things without a bit of nagging? What would *that* do to the stress level in our homes? How would that impact our energy level each day?

Oh, I was excited now! For the first time since we became aware of our parenting problems, I could see a solution and sense a bit of hope. *This felt good.*

By the time Mark came home that evening, I was ready to talk it through. He had ideas to add to our individual lists and we hatched a plan for how to tell the children about this new system we were putting into play. But first, we needed to build it.

Once we completed the lists of tasks for our children, we wrote each item on a Popsicle stick. We stated them simply and used pictures for the children who could not yet read. Initially, we limited the number of tasks for each day: ten for our younger two and twenty for the school-aged kids. This would allow them time to adjust to our new plan and make it feel achievable. We put the sticks in the restaurant cups and labeled the cups with our kids' names.

That night at dinner, we held a family meeting. While our children ate, we explained that things had been rather difficult in our family for some time. We talked about how smart they all were and how they were able to do so many things. We talked about how we didn't want to nag at them, that it felt bad to us and felt bad to them and it didn't really work. We explained that we wanted to find a new way, *for them*, so that they would not be frustrated and so that they could do the things that were important to them. And then we handed out the cups.

Kids are funny. Before we could tell them anything more, they wanted to jump right in. They couldn't wait to look at the Sticks and do whatever was written on each one. They were excited because we couched the system in words and ideas they could understand. There was no, "Since you will not even get dressed without being told ..." or "Because your room is always such a horrible mess ...." Instead, we tried, "This will be so great for you because you will not need to be told ... because you will get to choose ... because it will help us to relax ...."

They quickly understood, and to them, the whole thing looked like fun. We told them they had to do *every stick, every day* and that it was good *for them*. We explained that they were allowed to choose when they did each stick. We knew that allowing that choice might be hard for us – what if one of them chose to get dressed after dinner? Or brush his teeth twice at noon? But, on the other hand, what if the directions we had been giving them about when to get dressed and when to clear the table were ones they agreed with? What if we didn't need to say it because they would choose a reasonable path anyway? We decided to give that a shot. We decided that maybe some of what we had been teaching might be saved up inside and ready for use.

The kids were excited. And the autonomy of it all, the maturity of it, the respectfulness of it, made them smile. They grabbed their cups with gusto and begged to begin right then.

Maybe you don't think that will happen for you. Or maybe you're worried about what will happen after the sheen wears off and putting a stick in a cup is no longer enough incentive for your little ones. Maybe there needs to be more.

It's a good thing that there is.

Parenting Pause:

1. Reflect on the goals you have for your kids. What are 10-20 things you would like them to do daily? Make a written list.

2. As you review your list, be intentional about what will be included. Address areas of struggle (timely bedtime, healthy snacks, cleaning up) and add them to the list. Teaching autonomy in these areas will relieve stress in your family.

3. Brainstorm things your kids love to do. Add these to the daily list.

Sticks Resources:

Our initial Stick list for our preschoolers (ages 2 & 3):

- Get dressed
- Clear dishes
- Read a book
- Play outside
- Take a nap
- Clean up
- Brush your teeth
- Play with your big brother

Our initial Stick list for our school-aged kids (ages 7 and 8):

- Get up on time
- Make / strip bed
- Get dressed
- Eat breakfast
- Clean breakfast
- Brush teeth

- Pack a healthy snack
- Get out school stuff
- Leave for school on time
- Have a snack
- Put away school stuff
- Play outside
- Do homework
- Practice piano
- Practice sport
- Clean room / closet for 5 minutes
- Help Mom
- Read 15 minutes
- Take a shower
- Lay out clothes
- Brush teeth
- Go to bed on time
- Play with your little sibling

Chapter Four: The Golden Stick

"Tell me and I forget,
teach me and I may remember,
involve me and I learn."
-Benjamin Franklin

When we started the system, it didn't seem like anything more was needed. The kids were happy and driven. Things began to change in our house. Shoes were put away, teeth were brushed, children were dressed, and I was happy. But how long would that last?

Mark and I knew that the wonder of this new system would quickly fade. We *knew* these little people with whom we shared a home. A shiny, new toy is fun -- for a while. But as time goes by, it is easy to lose interest and let things slide.

This, we did not want. There had to be a way to help our children stay motivated enough to continue with this new way.

So Mark and I introduced one small change that would hook our kids for good. We wanted to offer one more detail that would keep them working and playing and practicing and connecting for months and years to come.

What was our big idea? What magical item could accomplish all of this, and so much more?

It was ... a stick!

Ahh, but no ordinary stick. No, this stick was special, this stick was gold! (But sticking to our original goals of building an accessible and inexpensive system, it was really just a regular Popsicle stick, spray painted gold.)

The Golden Stick was the key. The Golden Stick was the element that caused my children, with all of their different personalities, to react to this system with equal enthusiasm. Because with the addition of the Golden Stick, they had a goal. They had a motivator. They had a reason to keep on keeping on.

When we showed the children the stack of shiny gold sticks, their faces lit up. Even in this time of over-entertainment and over-stimulation, a Popsicle stick painted gold is an amazing sight. They wanted it. They reached for it. We set it just outside their grasp.

"You see," we began, "if you do all your Sticks today, you can earn one of these! And do you know what it can do?"

They stared at us blankly and awaited the answer.

"With this," we continued, "you can earn the things you like. You can work toward special time with mom, your favorite meal, an outing with dad, or a toy that you choose. But you must earn it. Every day, if you do all your sticks, you may get a Golden Stick from Mom or Dad. Do you know how much a Golden Stick is worth?"

My four sweet children shook their heads and did not look away. In my hand, I held it still -- the Golden Stick. The thing they wanted.

"One Golden Stick is not worth much. But if you save them up and you get ten, you can trade them in for what you want."

We waited. They thought.

Noah raised his hand. "Could we go out for breakfast? Just me and you?"

Now the wheels were turning.

"Could we have my favorite dinner?"

"Could I buy a set of Legos?"

"Could my baby get a bottle?"

Mark and I smiled at each other. We nodded our heads, and our children ran out to do whatever Sticks they had left. They had a way to work toward what they valued, and we had motivation. A change was coming to our humble home.

So, maybe your child is a skeptic. Maybe your child is stubborn, is frustrated, is bored, is lazy, is confused. Maybe you think it cannot work. But, I will tell you *it can*. Because in my house, we have:

- A driven, rule-abiding, success-seeking, sweet firstborn who loves to settle into whatever he believes is right.
- A spirited, creative, passionate second-born who seeks to blaze a new trail and find the funny in whatever it is he does.
- A quiet, patient, slow-moving, easy-going third-born who is content to sit quite still and lose himself in thought.
- A strong-willed, highly verbal, toe (or whole foot) over-the-line, competitive, challenging fourth-born who is loving and fun and silly.

And they all do Sticks.

Also, we know families with many kids and families with few kids and families with impaired kids and families with autistic kids and families with kids who fight and families with kids who obey and families with kids who don't. And they all do Sticks.

And it works.

Because the children get it. And because the Golden Stick makes it matter to them.

And while your children focus on what matters to them, you are teaching them something else. You are teaching them that what they want can be *earned.* That there is value in work well-done. That momma and daddy hear them and value their say in the world.

That, they get.

And for that, they are willing to put away their shoes.

Without ever being told again.

Parenting Pause:

1. What are some things that your children value? Is it possible to make these goals toward which your children can work?

2. Do any of your children need special encouragement as they begin the Sticks program? Which child? In what area?

3. What stumbling blocks do you foresee in planning for the "spending of Sticks"? How can you creatively plan around such areas?

Sticks Resources:

Appropriate uses for the "spending" of 10 Golden Sticks:

1. A pack of trading cards. We used Pokémon cards when my children were little. I bought them in bulk packages and kept them on hand.
2. A favorite meal and perhaps the opportunity to make that meal with a parent.
3. Time alone with a parent.
4. A small Lego product. I bought these on sales and had them available when someone had saved 10 sticks.
5. A baby bottle for a doll.
6. Arts and crafts time.
7. Extra screen time.
8. A playdate with friends.

Some creative ideas:

1. A family with a child on the autism spectrum decided to use Sticks to reinforce the internalizing of daily tasks. This child loved trains. He traded his 10 Sticks for a trip to a local city on a train. He only valued the travel time, so once they arrived downtown, they returned home on the next train.

2. Another family had an animal-loving son, but no pets of their own. This child saved his 10 Sticks to earn a playdate at his house with the pet of a family friend.

3. Another family, who regularly enforced Saturday cleaning chores, let their children save their Sticks for a coupon that allowed them to "pass" on one chore during that time. While this made more work for the parents on the weekends, there was less to do since the weekly tasks had been enthusiastically accomplished.

Chapter Five: Discipline

*"Treat a child as though he is already
the person he is capable of becoming."
-Haim Ginott*

Very quickly, our family life began to take on a rhythm that was comforting to all of us. I was grateful to find that necessary chores were being accomplished, and my children were beginning to take responsibility for what they needed to do each day. Our Sticks journey had begun with the depressing realization that our kids were not internalizing the many lessons we were seeking to teach them. Finding them taking age-appropriate responsibility was refreshing and encouraging.

I could sense the release of built-up tension and began to find that I had more energy. Before starting Sticks, we spent much of our day correcting and directing the life of our young family. The space this took in my head was overwhelming and exhausting. Once we found a way for our children to manage their activities and chores, I was freed up to be the momma I had always wanted to be. I was available to cuddle with my children. I had the attention to offer when homework was hard and days were dismal. I had the energy to invite a child to make dinner with me, to sit still and hear a well-practiced concerto, to listen deeply to a tale of school-aged drama. It was almost overwhelming as I began to realize all I had been missing due to the way I managed our family. Distraction and stress had cost me so much!

While the organization and structure of Sticks was helping, our life was not without issues. We did still live with four young children! In the midst of chores accomplished, books read, and connections made, there were discipline issues that reared their ugly heads. We began to be more aware of:

- tendencies to talk back, often in disrespectful tones
- truths untold or outright lying

- tantrums that flew so out of control that our intervention was necessary to calm them down
- quiet disobedience that often went unnoticed

Maybe these things had been there all along. Maybe we were just now able to take notice of the things that our children were doing. But now that we were aware, we needed to pay new attention to discipline and improve the methods we use to correct.

But how?

When we first began Sticks, Mark and I agreed that once a Stick is earned, it is yours to keep. We felt strongly that our children were working hard for their reward and that the system was working miracles in our home. We did not want our children to face losing Sticks because they were so hard won.

What an idealistic way to look at it all! What we were missing was that we now had a way to motivate our kids toward behavior that we felt was respectful and appropriate. They loved the Sticks and were saving up Golden Sticks like misers! This way of approaching the structure of our family life had offered us a new and powerful currency. Though we did not want to use the Sticks as a measure of discipline in a haphazard way, we did begin to understand that we could use it to teach our children to control their behavior independently. After all, one of our favorite things about the program was that any future lessons for our children could be easily dealt with by tacking on additional Sticks. Could lessons also be addressed by taking away Sticks?

When looking at the misbehavior of children, Mark and I found that most actions deal directly with either their mouths or their ears. For instance:

- When I tell a child to go check their Sticks cup, and they do not move to follow that direction, they are not listening. Ear.
- When I ask for a hand in preparing dinner or setting the table and I hear, "C'mon, Mom! I helped you yesterday! How come you never ask Noah?" they are showing verbal disrespect. Mouth.

- When, in a moment of anger, one of my children hits another child, they are ignoring family rules and not listening to what we have taught. Ear.
- When an unkind word flies from one sibling to another, belittling or bullying that child, words are misused and become weapons. Mouth.

Think it through. When your children misbehave, into what category does it fall? Are they not listening? Talking back? Using mean words? Ignoring expectations? Who knew that our ears and our mouths were so powerful?

Because we were becoming aware of a greater need for discipline, this clarification was helpful to us. And in understanding this, we were able to create a strong addition to our Sticks system.

Using simple online clip-art (see the end of this chapter for examples), we made each child three Mouth cards and three Ear cards, laminated for endurance. We put these Mouths and Ears onto a poster board, using Velcro, and set the board out in a central location in our home. Each child had a column labeled with his or her name and showing three Mouths and three Ears below that name. Now we were getting somewhere!

As Mark and I talked through our new idea, we knew that we wanted it to be very hard to lose a Golden Stick. We wanted our kids to be successful, and so we decided that you could only lose a Golden Stick if you lost three Mouths OR three Ears in one given day. (A combination of these would not lead to a loss.) With a plan in place, we put the board out for the kids to contemplate.

When the children noticed the poster board, they had many, many questions. Leaving them in their curiosity, we planned a family meeting.

That night at dinner, we offered an explanation.

"You are all doing such a great job with Sticks, and we know you love saving up for things that are important to you," we told them. "We are so proud of how hard you are working and all the things you are getting accomplished each day. We feel so much better, and we know you do too. We want to find more and more ways to live nicely together."

We talked about how we all want to use our mouths and our ears better. We all want to listen well and to speak carefully. We explained that being respectful in our tone and our words is important, and that we wanted to speak calmly and respectfully to them, too.

The kids were excited about the prospect of getting along better but unsure about how often they might be corrected. When they realized that they ran the risk of losing a Golden Stick, they were worried.

Because we believe in preparing our kids to meet expectations, we told them we would give them a week to understand the Mouths and Ears before they would risk losing a Stick.

For the next week, we offered verbal warnings about behaviors we wanted them to correct. When someone ignored a parental direction, we calmly reminded them that next week, that choice would result in "pulling an Ear" off the chart. And losing an Ear or Mouth also meant they would be given an extra chore and be closer to losing a Golden Stick. We followed the same process to teach them to use their words more carefully and to respond to us and to one another with greater respect.

After a week, we were ready to begin. The transition was easy and smooth. They were so in love with the Golden Sticks by this time that they were willing to use greater self-control. From time to time, someone would lose an Ear or a Mouth, *and then they would self-correct*. We watched one child speak disrespectfully to another, lose a mouth and then make a concerted effort to use kind language throughout the rest of the day. The Golden Stick was so deeply desired that they were willing to make changes to maintain their stash.

Mark and I were thrilled to see a new level of maturity rising out of our young children. We had been struggling with placing external demands on their behavior, but those expectations now came from within. The teaching we had offered them was taking root, and we could see the fruit.

It was a tremendous relief! And while all our days were not perfect, we had enough hope to strengthen us for the tougher times.

It was weeks before anyone lost a Golden Stick. And when it finally did occur, it was in the midst of a tantrum gone awry.

Two of our kids feel emotions passionately, which, for them, also meant a tendency toward tantrums. For years we had struggled with helping them to settle down when things got out of control. Mark and I were consistently drawn into the drama and often had to physically hold a child to make the tantrum stop. It was exhausting, and it did not teach our children to calm themselves.

Now, we were learning a new way. All of us. In the midst of an impending tantrum, we learned to find our calmest voice and quietly say, "I would like you calm down now. You would like to calm down, too. I know you do not want to lose a Golden Stick. So let's settle down so you do not lose any more Mouths or Ears."

And it did not take long before this began to work.

For the first time in our parenting years, we were all speaking the same language. We were all on the same page. The release of stress and anxiety was palpable, and we all felt a renewed sense of hope. Because we were not locked in a power struggle over chores, expectations, or behavior, we were newly available to parent our children in a better way. We were able to come alongside them in the midst of difficult days, teaching them calmly when something was new or needed to be changed. We found ourselves finally able to focus on their stories, their lives, their growth.

And all of this brought a new joy and peace to our shared life.

Where would we go from here?

Parenting Pause:

1. What difficult behaviors would you like to see your children change? Make a list of these behaviors.

2. Looking at the list above, mark each behavior as a Mouth or an Ear. If the behavior comes from not listening or not obeying a given direction or rule, it is an Ear. If the behavior is verbal, like using unkind words or being disrespectful, it is a Mouth.

3. Plan an encouraging family meeting to go over this understanding of behavior. How can you build up your children as you seek to correct them?

Sticks Resources:

Chapter Six: The Big Picture

"We cannot always build the future for our youth,
but we can build our youth for the future."
-Franklin D. Roosevelt

It has been nearly a decade since that morning that changed our lives. And even as I sit here, I can remember every detail of that ordinary day. I can remember where I stood when Benjamin looked at me calmly and responded to my stuttered question with, "You didn't tell us to."

Our children are older now, and I can see the impact of the Sticks system on them. We have lived through many seasons together, and this tool has offered us the structure we needed. We have been able to help them internalize the life lessons we wanted to give them.

As we work through life with our four, we are more and more convinced that it is easy to lose your way when you believe that your goal is to raise good children. Parenting is not about raising good kids.

It is, instead, about raising our children to become good adults.

When we buy into the fallacy of raising good kids, we find ourselves seeking short-term wins. We become distracted by appearances and habits. We may prioritize playdates, activities, and the picture-perfect life we wrongly believe exists. The problem comes when our kids begin to grow up, and we suddenly realize that we were never going to reach this goal.

When we choose a big-picture focus, it is easier to believe that all the little decisions we make today will add up to life-long lessons. And it's easier to remember that every single time we choose not to teach the hard lesson, we are losing the opportunity to help our kids learn what they must.

When I speak to parents about this topic, I always have someone tell me that it is just "easier to do it myself" than to require a child to clean up their dishes, put away their toys, or handle household chores. And while I want to choose gentle words, I must be truthful. This work, the parenting of our children, is not about finding the path that is easiest for us. No. Instead, this is a time for us to dream about where our children are headed and to prepare them to live the life that is to come. It is a time for us to decide what tasks are appropriate for our kids and to teach them how to do them. It is a time for us to instill in them a work ethic that will allow them take care of themselves and others, to earn what they value, to land in well-balanced lives that include work and play, faith and family, activity and rest. And if we leave our kids in a place where all of the effort comes from us instead of from them, they may flounder as they leave the nest, unsure how to structure a life.

These days of hands-on parenting must be done in a loving and gracious way that keeps on eye on what is to come. Because an empty nest may feel like it is a lifetime away, but I can tell you confidently that it is not.

I live with a boy who is about to turn 18. When he looks at me from across the room, the face I see is still the one he had when he began school. Sometimes, he laughs and throws his head back and I can see years of happy moments in that one act. I am stunned that in a few short months, he will walk across the stage at his high school graduation. And a few short months after that, he will head off to college.

And I know, for certain, that there were days when this moment felt really far away. There were seasons that felt like forever. There were long days when I was weary and did not know if we were heading in a way that would matter at all.

But from where I stand today, all of those moments were no more than a blink. All of those memories can so quickly collapse on top of one another, and I find myself hoping that we have taught him enough. I want him to be prepared and *to feel* prepared for all that is to come. And from this place, I can honestly say that I never had enough time.

Never.

Do you see? We do not have the luxury of making choices based on what is easiest for us. We have been given these children and the task at hand. And we have limited days to help them begin to live out the goals we have for them and the goals they will make for themselves.

So, we need a plan.

For us, Sticks offered the structure we needed to put our goals in action. And while accomplishing chores was a part of it, it was never meant to be the whole. Sticks assists your kids to internalize your teaching. It gives you a way to bring into each day those things you believe are important.

Using Sticks, our kids became life-long learners and readers. Because it was a part of what we valued, it became a daily habit and a way for them to work toward things they wanted while learning to love literature.

Using Sticks, our kids learned to value outdoor play. Because we prioritized this over technology, our four spent hours outdoors regularly and have a deep love for nature and creative play.

Using Sticks, our kids learned that they have a role to play in family life. Because we share the tasks that need to be done daily, our kids do not believe that household work is the job of an adult. They see that it takes all of us to create a home that runs smoothly. And they gladly participate in this work.

Using Sticks, our kids learned to connect with one another and to see the importance in this bond. For years, they have been spending time together daily, doing what the other wanted to do. They learned that being in relationship means that you do not always get your way, that loving someone else means you give importance to the things that *they* find important.

Using Sticks, our kids learned about living in healthy ways. Mark and I were able to free ourselves from the power struggle over fruits and veggies. Sticks helped our kids choose good snacks, participate in gardening, and pack healthy treats for their lunches.

Using Sticks, our kids realized that when your home life is stressful, everyone can work together to find a better way. They learned that we all play a part in this. Because of this, it is difficult for them to vilify Mark and me when we must offer discipline and correction. This has led us to healthy relationships as they have grown up. When things are running smoothly at home, when parents do not have to micro-manage every detail of every life, we are offered lots of room to connect, to communicate, to care.

The lessons we have learned are endless. And it is a relief to think that our children are growing up and out with all this under their belts. I do not know if I will ever feel like we have taught them enough. But I know that we have done all that we can to help them to save up and own the many things we have taken the time to teach. I believe this will surely matter.

And this momma finds deep peace in that knowledge.

Parenting Pause:

1. Do you feel you are choosing the path that is easiest for you? In what areas?

2. What would make it easier for you to hand over tasks to your children?

3. What things do you feel you are teaching well? What areas could you do a better job of addressing?

Conclusion

"Our greatest weakness lies in giving up.
The most certain way to succeed
is to always try just one more time."
-Thomas A. Edison

So, what will you do next? You sit with a choice before you. You can fall into bed at the end of this day and get up tomorrow to begin it all again. The same.

Get up. Get by. Get to bed. Repeat.

Or you can find another path. You can decide today that there is hope for less stress and more peace, less struggle and more teaching. You can choose that tomorrow will not be a repeat but will be a whole new thing.

Got Sticks?

You need to find time to get some Popsicle sticks and you need to do it soon. Lots of people read books. You want more than that.

So, get to a store and buy some Sticks, but do not waste your time and money on that little baggie they sell. Do not be distracted by the colorful bags of rainbow balsam! Instead, find the big box of Popsicle sticks that is overflowing with possibilities. Inside you will find 1,000 sticks, and you will not have to go back anytime soon for more. And while you are out driving, brainstorm a list of things your kids do every day. This is an amazing start!

Once you are home, write down those tasks. (If you need a place to start, our lists were included in Chapter 3.) You do not need to make them long. You want to encourage your kids and empower them to be able to complete their Sticks in a single day.

You know what to do from here. Tasks on Sticks. Place in cups. Plan a family meeting.

When you pitch this idea to your kids, remember to keep it positive. You are offering a new path that will reduce stress and give them a chance to work toward things that matter to them. This is a new *opportunity*. And it is going to be *great!*

From that point, just watch for change. It is coming. Your children will respond. Stay positive and encouraging and watch things fall into place.

When we began this program, I wanted to fix what was broken. I had no idea what would come of it all. I still shake my head in disbelief. This was never supposed to be a topic to speak on. It was never going to be a book. I started this system to save my family, because I knew that we were missing the mark and I wanted to offer more. I had no idea that a plastic cup and a handful of Popsicle sticks could transform our lives so completely.

But it did.

And the same can happen for you.

This is a good time to begin.

Addendum: Common Questions about Sticks

"It's not what you do for your kids,
but what you teach them to do for themselves,
that will make them successful human beings."
-JM Power

I have been speaking about this topic for years. As I have traveled from group to group, conference to conference, I have been asked many questions about the system. Here are the questions I hear most often:

How do Sticks work in practice?

In the morning, our children spill their cup of Sticks onto the table and lay out the Sticks in the order they would like to do them. If they have any Golden Sticks, they put those back into the cup.

Our school-aged children have Sticks that have been colored green on the very top of edge of the Stick. These green tips are easily seen when looking at the Sticks in the cup due to this marking. All of these green-tipped Sticks are "morning Sticks" and must be done before school. The rest of the Sticks are "afternoon Sticks" and can be done before bedtime. (Keep in mind that if you have a repeated task, such as Brush Teeth that will need to be done in the morning and in the evening, you may put two Sticks into the cup, marking one for AM and one for PM.)

As they complete a Stick, they pop it back into the cup. When *all* their Sticks are back in the cup, they are done! If they finish every Stick in a day, they earn a Golden Stick. They can request this from either parent at a time when that parent is near the cup that holds the Golden Sticks. We keep this cup in our kitchen, on top of the fridge.

Where do you keep the Sticks cups?

We have tried many locations for the cups, including the kitchen island, our bay window, the coffee table, and the piano bench. I am partial to the piano bench because it is easily hidden if we need to quickly clean up.

A family in the Midwest recently told me that they attached tiny magnets to their Sticks and keep them on the fridge. Great idea! Another family keeps the Sticks and cups on a cookie sheet so it can easily be moved to a convenient location. Whether you have a tiny living space or plenty of room, there are ways to tweak this system to work for you!

How do you know which Stick belongs to which child?

Ideally, you will not even have to worry about this. Because your children are in charge of their own Stick Cups, you should not have to keep track of Sticks. However, life with children can be full. In our family, after the Stick Cups fell on the floor a couple of times, we knew we needed to make an adjustment to quickly be able to refill each cup with the correct child's Sticks.

Now, when I am writing Sticks, I also put the child's initial at the opposite end of the Stick. This way, if I find a Stick on the floor at any point, I can pop it back into the correct cup.

What do you do if your child is not able to wait to earn 10 Sticks?

There is a lot of grace available in this system. The idea is to make it work for your family. And you are the expert on them! You need to find a way to make it enticing for an impatient or very young child. If this means that they will earn something for 5 Golden Sticks instead of 10, do that! Over time you can extend the number of Sticks it takes to earn whatever they are working toward. But you want to make it accessible. You want it to be encouraging. You want to help them to learn to love the Golden Stick. When this happens, you will have a currency to help them learn other things and to encourage them to control their behavior.

If you have more than one child, please know that you have access to a powerful teaching tool! The impact of "positive peer pressure" cannot be overlooked. If all of your children are using Sticks and working to earn things they value, a resistant child will see siblings receive rewards while he/she stubbornly waits you out.

Do not give in! Remind yourself that fair does not mean that all your children get the same thing. *Fair means that everyone gets what they need.* That is an important distinction. Offer encouragement to all your children as they learn to use this system. Make the rewards available quickly. But never offer a reward to a child who has not yet met the goal that you have set. When they learn that you will actually make them gather those Golden Sticks, they are also learning that you are a person of your word. More importantly, they are learning that doing a job well results in meeting a goal. What an important life lesson!

Can I put my spouse on Sticks?

That is a different book!

What do you do if you have a day where your schedule makes it impossible to finish all the Sticks?

Grace upon grace. You offer that. You have to remember that while this system makes accomplishing tasks possible, doing chores is not the point of Sticks. The point is teaching our kids the lessons they need to internalize and carry into adulthood. So, on busy days in our house we may tell our kids that they only need to do a few Sticks. We will give them a pass on the rest and be understanding about time constraints. We want to keep the important things important. Teaching. Preparing. These are our goals.

Are your teens still on Sticks?

Several years after we started this system, I had an interesting exchange with Noah, my oldest. It was a summer morning, and I reminded the kids to check their Sticks. Noah started to walk toward his cup when he turned and looked at me.

He said, "Mom, it's the weirdest thing. I know what my Sticks all say without laying them out. I can get them all done just by remembering what I do each day. I don't really need to use them."

Mission accomplished.

As my kids' needs change, how we use Sticks changes. Our teens no longer rely on the system as they once did. But the point of Sticks was not to create a system to use forever. It was to *teach our kids*.

That said, if things in our house begin to fall apart a bit, we always come back to Sticks to renew the structure that keeps our home running well.

If you are beginning this system for the first time and have teens in your home, I would recommend that you talk with them before starting and allow them to feel like they are a part of the process. Since building age-appropriate autonomy is a goal of the system, this is a helpful approach.

Perhaps they would like to use physical Popsicle Sticks or perhaps they have another idea. When they feel like you are offering them respect in this choice, you will have far fewer issues with their cooperation.

How old do my kids need to be to start Sticks?

When we started Sticks, Noah and Benjamin were 7 and 8. Josiah and Elizabeth were 3 and 2. We decided to start them all at the same time because we knew that our littlest ones loved to do whatever their big brothers were doing. With very young kids, we are teaching a process more than teaching the tasks on the Sticks. We are teaching them how to take age-appropriate responsibility for small things. While Noah and Benjamin could do most of their Sticks independently, we had to come alongside Josiah and Elizabeth and do the tasks with them.

We also put images on the Sticks for our little ones, instead of words. For play outside, we drew a tree. For brush teeth, we drew a smile. There was nothing fancy about our program. We wanted it to be simple and accessible and this worked well. Ball point pen on Popsicle stick. That is as fancy as we got.

How can I use Sticks to foster connection between my children?

We have used Sticks to encourage "cross-play" between our kids of different ages.

Start by giving an older child a Stick with the name of a younger sibling on it. In the beginning, our older sons would ask their younger sibling, "Would you like to play?"

In our experience, when a little sister is asked by her older brother to play, she will always say, "Yes!"

We taught our older boys to ask, "What would you like to do?" They would then spend 15 minutes with their younger sibling doing that activity, even if it was an undesirable activity to them. We taught them that the relationship they were building with their sibling was worth more than their desire to do something else.

Since we have four kids, these became our first "switching" Sticks, where the sibling Sticks were switched among the older boys each week. (One week Noah would play with Josiah and Benjamin would play with Elizabeth, the next week they'd switch off.)

As the kids grew up, we continued to offer them a multitude of ways to work and play together in hopes of creating connections that would strengthen over time. Sticks grow with your family!

Can Sticks reduce power struggles over food?

One of our goals is to teach our kids to live healthy lives, which we define as being active (playing outside and being involved in a sport) and choosing healthy, natural food.

We have kids who are picky eaters and we wanted to let ourselves out of this battle. To do this, we stopped buying food that we did not want them to eat. Parents have far more control over this than we often believe. Kids cannot eat what we do not provide.

We do allow for some treats. We find that our kids are happy to eat fruit, yogurt, nuts, and granola knowing that sometimes they get chocolate, too.

Over time, we added a "healthy snack" Stick for after school and for packed lunches. Because the only treats we have are those that we are comfortable with, these are the snacks that are packed.

(As an aside, we do not make special meals for kids who choose not to eat what we cook, and we do set expectations that they eat what we provide. We also have served unfinished dinners for breakfast- but only once to each child. This is a powerful lesson!)

Is any age too old to begin?

This book offers you a structure. How can you adjust this to work for your child? How can you meet them where they are so that you can reduce stress in your home? How can you empower them to work toward something they value while internalizing the lessons you are offering? I do not believe that kids age out of Sticks, but you may need to adjust how you use it to work with your older child. Create higher expectations, raise the number of Sticks needed for a reward, and increase the value of the things they can earn. (Some ideas: a new article of clothing, hosting a friend overnight, choosing a restaurant for just the two of you.)

We get a lot of messages from our culture telling us that teens are difficult and selfish. This message can become a self-fulfilling prophecy. *It does not have to be this way.* When we build strong relationships with our kids, we can enjoy delightful relationships with them through their teen years. We need to raise the bar high and expect them to respectful and loving. And then that is what they will do. They want to please you, even when it seems this is not the case. So talk it through with them and make a plan that will use the base of this system to create positive change for your family. It is possible. I live with two teens and two tweens. I know this to be true.

Does the Golden Stick have a monetary value?

In short, no. When we began this system, I would buy things I knew my kids valued and keep them on hand for purchase with Golden Sticks. Ten sticks would equal one special item. I purposely did not attach a monetary value because I loved to shop sales and would save money on items I kept on hand.

When the kids got older and wanted to work toward bigger items, we offered them the opportunity to save up more than 10 Sticks to accomplish that goal. It began with a desire for bigger Lego sets, which can be pricey. We allowed them to save their Golden Sticks and set a desired number to purchase the set. This also gave us time to budget for these items. We really liked this since one of our original goals was to teach our kids to know what they value and save for things they want.

If you wanted to incorporate the Sticks system with an allowance plan in your family, you can. I would suggest $0.50 per Golden Stick for little ones and $1.00 for older kids.

Do I really have to spray paint Sticks?

Nope. You can visit my website and find a link to have Golden Sticks mailed to you. My website is http://nadiaswearingen-friesen.com/

How can I get more information about Sticks?

I am a national speaker with years of experience, and I love this topic. It is not only my most popular talk, but also one of my favorites to give. I am able and willing to travel to speak on this and many other parenting topics. You can find more information about booking me to speak near you by visiting my website at http://nadiaswearingen-friesen.com/. All my talks are encouraging and practical, and I love what I do.

Acknowledgements

From the beginning, this book has been a joint project and I am deeply aware that I could not have written this alone.

When we found ourselves asleep at the wheel, my husband Mark willingly brainstormed with me about ways we could get back on track. There is no way that Sticks would have ever come to be without his creativity. He helped me to remember the parents we wanted to be and fought with me to find our way back to a place that has allowed us to love our children the way we hoped we would. And as the details of this book consistently changed, he evaluated, edited, tweaked and clarified the story I sought to tell. I am so thankful for his support.

When Mark and I sat down at the table at our first Sticks family meeting, four young children joined us there. As different from one another as night and day, they taught me how this simple approach to structuring our family life might work for other families. I am so grateful to Noah, Benjamin, Josiah and Elizabeth for their enthusiastic love for all things Sticks! (And for being four of the most amazing kids I have ever met!) Being present to watch them grow and develop has meant the world to me.

Over the years, I have spoken to many groups, near and far, about this system. Their words of affirmation and curious responses have kept me going on this project when it seemed it would never get done. Every single time I spoke on Sticks, someone asked me for the book. I am so thankful for these requests and for the fire it lit in me to keep on working when discouragement set in.

As I have worked through the process of writing this book, so many people have affirmed my efforts. I heard from family near and far, friends and acquaintances, people who believed I could do this before I was sure. I wish I could gather you all into one place and thank you. I am grateful.

In the final stages of completing this text, there were folks who joined the process in such key ways. I am so thankful to Sarah Zylstra, my editor. Even when other pressures vied for her attention, she found a way to continue working with me on Sticks. I honestly do not believe I could have completed the work without her consistent voice and gracious direction.

And lastly, I will forever be grateful to the team of people who agreed to help me launch this book. They read and questioned. They experimented with the system. They willing walked alongside me as I watched a Word document on my laptop become a book. If you have heard about Sticks, you can thank them, too. The way they shared this information with others, all over the world, is nothing short of phenomenal. Thank you, Team. You are the best.

From the Author

I'd love to hear how this book has encouraged you personally. You can find me online easily. On my website – www.NadiaSwearingen-Friesen.com – you can drop me a note, locate additional resources on my Sticks page, read my latest blog, and check out my speaking topics and upcoming events. You can also follow me on these social media sites:

Facebook: www.Facebook.com/nadialisesf

Twitter: @NadiaLise

Instagram: NadiaLiseSF

Pinterest: NadiaLise

Whether I hear from you or not, I wish you blessings and perseverance in your family's journey. *Stick* to it … you can do it!

Nadia

Made in the USA
San Bernardino, CA
28 March 2016